THE BIBLICAL ELDER:
FIRST A LEADER IN MINISTRY,
THEN AN ELDER

RICHARD SWARTLEY

RIGHT START PUBLICATIONS

Published by:
Right Start Publications, LLC
9952 Silver Maple Road
Highlands Ranch, CO 80129–5461
rightstart@aol.com

All Scripture quotations, unless otherwise indicated, are taken from the NEW AMERICAN STANDARD BIBLE ®, Copyright © 1960, 1962, 1963, 1968, 1971, 1972, 1973, 1975, 1977, 1995 by the Lockman Foundation. Used by permission.

Library of Congress Cataloging-in-Publication Data

Swartley, Richard H., 1934
The biblical elder: *first* a leader in ministry, *then* an elder
Richard H. Swartley
    Includes bibliographical references and indexes.
    ISBN 978-0-9817875-6-5
Church governance. 2. Church officers. 4. Elders. I. Title.

Printed in the United States of America

Contents

Acknowledgements

We are very grateful for our dear brother, Alexander Strauch, author of *Biblical Eldership* (see *Biblicaleldership.com*). He encouraged us to coauthor *The Mentor's Guide to Biblical Eldership* in 1996. The research for that project opened our eyes to the Biblical material on eldership and to the many implementation issues facing the church today.

Also, for her help in all aspects of this project, I thank my wife Anne. Because of her commitment to the Lord, her contributions and editing have been invaluable. This work demonstrates the effect of her loving encouragement and probing questions.

Our Calling

The Measure of a Church

Isn't it tragic that in many of our churches our people are primarily spectators, passive pew-sitters? They are not actively serving! Many congregations, both large and small—even those which are evangelical—are mere social gatherings where religious experience is provided by worship leaders and teams, and inspirational preaching. Even worse, as Douglas Groothuis has warned:

> The use of contemporary music and drama in worship can *diminish* the appreciation of God's transcendent holiness, especially if it is presented as a performance for spectators instead of an offering to God (italics added).[1]

For many churchgoers, their only active involvement is in showing up and maybe contributing to the budget that supports the venue and staff.

Ed Stetzer of the Billy Graham Center for Evangelism has issued this wake-up call:

> One of the reasons churches are stuck and stagnant is because they have for years pandered to the consumerist mentality of Christians. Then we're shocked and surprised when people act like customers rather than co-laborers.[2]

OUR CALLING

This is *not* what the apostles envisioned and set down for us through the Holy Spirit in their New Testament writings. The apostles made it clear that, in addition to living openly redeemed lives, the members of the family of God are to serve one another and the unsaved world. Instead of following the clear Biblical teaching to be making disciples, many of us have either isolated ourselves from the culture around us or conformed to its values and standards. In 2018 the Barna Research Group reported the alarming statistics that 51 percent of churchgoers have never heard of the Great Commission (Matt. 28:19–20), and only 17 percent are familiar with its meaning.[3]

The measure of the church that is true to New Testament intent is *not* the vibrancy of its Sunday morning worship service, the success of its charismatic preacher, or how large its congregation. The assessment of its spiritual health—and whether it has fulfilled its calling—are demonstrated by the *degree* to which its members are serving—that is, personally ministering to one another and to those outside the church who urgently need their witness.

If lack of participation in true service is the case, this may not be the members' fault. This problem is usually caused unintentionally by the wrong kind of, or inadequate, leadership. It may even be the logical result of failed leadership. So, we need to evaluate ourselves. Are our priorities those of the Apostles? Are they God-given?

- Paul instructed the Ephesians: "We are *His workmanship*, created in Christ Jesus *for good works*, which God prepared beforehand so that *we would walk in them*" (2:10, italics added).

- In Romans he elaborated: "So we, who are many, are one body in Christ, and individually members one of another. Since *we have gifts* that differ according to the grace given to us, *each of us is to exercise them* accordingly" (12:5–6, italics added).

- For the Galatians Paul summarized: *"Bear one another's burdens*, and thereby fulfill the law of Christ" (6:2), and "So then, while we have opportunity, *let us do good to all people,* and especially to those who are of the household of the faith" (6:10, italics added).

- James made our responsibilities explicit and practical: "If a brother or sister is without clothing and in need of daily food, and one of you says to them, 'Go in peace, be warmed and be filled,' and yet you do not *give them what is necessary* for their body, what use is that?" (2:15–16, italics added).

- And: "Pure and undefiled religion in the sight of our God and Father is this: to *visit orphans and widows* in their distress" (James 1:27, italics added).

- John stressed the same point: "But whoever has the world's goods, and sees his brother in need and closes his heart against him, *how does the love of God abide in him*?" (1 John 3:17, italics added).

The Lord's charge to His chosen family is crystal clear—serve one another. The question is, How do we take up His challenge? Who will teach us how to use our God-given gifts in serving one another? Who is supposed to lead by example? Are there models to be emulated?

Biblical Eldership

The New Testament specifically designates *elders* to be the leaders responsible for Christ's church. These are the men charged with: "the equipping of the saints for the work of service, to the building up of the body of Christ" (Eph. 4:12). And the *true elder* is known by this qualification: He is a servant leader. If our elders do not exercise their personal leadership in our churches' ministries, our congregations will never be discipled, and then equipped, to take the gospel everywhere, as the Lord Jesus commanded:

> "Go therefore and *make disciples of all the nations*, baptizing them in the name of the Father and the Son and the Holy Spirit, teaching them to observe all that I commanded you; and lo, I am with you always, even to the end of the age" (Matt. 28:19–20, italics added).

The writings of men like Alexander Strauch (*Biblical Eldership*),[4] Joseph Hellerman (*Embracing Shared Leadership*),[5] Benjamin L. Merkle (*40 Questions About Elders and Deacons*),[6] and this author (*Eldership in Action*),[7] as well as such web resources offered by Curt Parton (*exploringthefaith.com*),[8] Daniel B. Wallace (*Who Should Run the Church? A Case for the Plurality of Elders, bible.org*),[9] John Piper (*A Biblical Examination of Key Terms,*)[10] and *biblicaleldership. com*,[11] have persuaded many of us that we must follow Paul's example: He "*appointed* elders for them in every church" (Acts 14:23, italics added). That is our Biblical pattern for governance of Christ's church.

Repeating the arguments for governance by elders and their required character qualities is not needed here since they are very clearly given in 1 Timothy 3 and Titus 1. Moreover, expert Biblical scholars and teachers have admirably explained these standards, setting forth in detail the necessary components. Many of us are now convinced that our churches are to be *governed by elders*.

But my question is this: Is it possible that, when we are examining and appointing men for eldership, we are underestimating, even ignoring, a *critical qualification* required in each man?

The Critical Qualification

We take seriously the Apostle Paul's instructions to Timothy: "Preach the word; be ready in season and out of season; reprove, rebuke, exhort, with great patience and instruction" (2 Tim. 4:2). These were not imperatives only for an apostolic delegate like Timothy. They remain God's requirements for His elders today. They must hold "fast the faithful Word which is in accordance with the teaching, so that [they] will be able both to exhort in sound doctrine and to refute those who contradict" (Titus 1:9). Steady attention to Biblical truth is paramount for the Church.

But because the New Testament emphasizes this essential gift of preaching and teaching, we often miss *a critical and essential qualification* of the true elder. Even though it is explicit in New Testament teaching, we have allowed it to be ignored. This neglected qualification is *the ability and readiness to lead, and the demonstration of leadership in active service.* In this book, we are specifically concerned with this leadership qualification.

There are significant differences between being gifted to teach or preach and being gifted to lead a ministry of the church. Preaching from a podium or teaching in any venue involves:

- Selecting the material to be taught, presumably based on the congregation's or group's needs;
- Clarifying the context and meaning of the Scripture text;
- Presenting Biblical truth in a way that is interesting, facilitates retention, and stimulates application in daily life.

Contrast this with service as the leader of a ministry of the church. In this role a man must:

- Possess a vision from the Lord for that ministry;
- Persuade others to share that vision;
- Recruit, train, and—especially—*shepherd* ministry participants;
- Actively demonstrate his love for the ministry's participants;
- Evaluate feedback, procedures, and results;
- Make any necessary adjustments.

The skill of teaching is different from the ability to lead in, or support, a ministry, and exceptional ability in both skills is rarely found combined in the same man. This fact is borne out in surveys of those who self-identify as pastors. Only 12 percent of senior pastors claim to have the gift of leadership, in contrast to 67 percent who claim to have the gift of teaching or preaching.[12]

Because of the importance of serving as leaders, it is no surprise that the requirements for elders given in 1 Timothy 3 and Titus 1 emphasize relationships. The overwhelming majority of the elder's essential qualities concern the candidate's integrity and leadership in personal interactions within his own family and in the body of believers—in other words, to his *servant leadership.* Even the traits of "addicted to wine" and "not a new convert" effect the elder's interpersonal relationships. One might argue that "able to teach" could be viewed in isolation from the man's relational interactions. But even that responsibility is coupled with "refut[ing] those who contradict," which involves interaction. In fact, what Paul did ask for is *leadership*:

> But we request of you, brethren, that you appreciate those who diligently *labor among you*, and *have charge over you* in the Lord and *give you instruction*, and that you esteem them very highly in love because of *their work* (1 Thess. 5:12–13, italics added).

What does this phrase, "have charge over you," mean? "Have charge over" is the translation of the same Greek word, *proïstēmi*, Paul used in 1 Timothy 5:17, where he wrote of the elders who "rule" well (in most translations). In many modern English translations of this passage this Greek word, *proïstēmi*, is consistently and misleadingly translated as "rule."

Gerhard Kittel and Gerhard Friedrich, editors of the *Theological Dictionary of the New Testament*, give the accurate meaning of *proïstēmi* as *"leading by virtue of being out in front of, or caring for, others."*[13] This meaning of *proïstēmi* is clearly distinguished from the leadership or management from one's position like the leading of a king or Chief Executive Officer (CEO). Paul could have used another word, *archō* (rule), but he did not. *Proïstēmi*, in contrast to *archō*, never implies a power relationship. Elders' genuine authority is truly demonstrated in their lovingly and humbly shepherding and caring for God's household. And the best use of the body's efforts and gifts, given by the Holy Spirit to the believers, requires servant leadership.

Because of the importance of serving as leaders, it is no surprise that the requirements for elders given in 1 Timothy 3 and Titus 1 emphasize relationships

---

The godly leader is known by his responsible actions, not his position. He discerns, and then steps up to address, a gap in the body's ministry. Moreover, this leader understands the art of motivating a group to achieve a common goal. He persuades and strengthens those he leads, giving them vision and courage as they work together.

The worthy leader does not lecture but speaks truth through asking penetrating questions. Being biblically astute, he is able to combat false assumptions without being overbearing. He knows how to stimulate, confront, solve conflicts, even ask for forgiveness, and bless. He sees potential in each volunteer, being generous with his attention and concern. He tries to speak the language of whatever unique assortment of believers the Lord brings to his team. He considers them resources entrusted to his stewardship, and prizes each as the Lord's work in progress.

Two Hindrances

The church has been hindered from obtaining real elders because of two interrelated problems. First, we have neglected leadership ability and initiative as critical qualifications when evaluating a man's suitability for eldership. Second, we have allowed the takeover of the church by professionals, thereby denying the men of our congregations opportunities to display their Holy Spirit-inspired leadership. Are we ignoring leadership aptitude to our peril?

Regrettably, the leadership in most churches has been made the responsibility of *staff*—"trained," salaried "professionals," and not the work of volunteers. Fundamentally, this practice is incompatible with Biblical eldership. If there are no opportunities to serve the Lord by leading for the men who may become elder candidates—the "equipped saints" of Ephesians 4:12—then it is not possible to evaluate their leadership skills, or their eligibility for eldership.

We have neglected leadership ability and initiative as critical qualifications when evaluating a man's suitability for eldership.

The use of staff for leadership in the church not only robs the body of shepherding by Holy Spirit-chosen men, but this practice deprives such men their privilege of serving Christ as His under-shepherds. A staff-led church, in which the major leadership is provided by non-elder professionals, is incompatible with plural Biblical eldership. So is hiring staff, and then appointing them as elders, whether or not they qualify. We have ignored these realities. The Lord has given His qualified *under-shepherds* "the work of service, to the building up of the body of Christ" (Eph. 4:12). At their best, staff-led structures allow only pseudo-biblical eldership. They actually prevent any desired or attempted transformation to leadership by Biblical elders.

Many churches want to, even try to, institute leadership by elders, but they fail or end up with seriously compromised versions. Why is implementation failure so frequent? Look at our history. Since the end of the first century, Christ's church has been hampered and corrupted because we borrowed from the surrounding secular cultures and structures, especially from those which catered to man's quest for power and control. The response to false teachers in the early churches was not increased, loving correction and instruction of the members by the elders. Instead it was the exercise of control and authority by bishops.[14]

A staff-led church, in which the major leadership is provided by non-elder professionals, is incompatible with plural Biblical eldership.

Even though the Reformation decisively restored the Biblical *theology* of salvation, it failed to reform the church's *governance*. John Calvin and Huldrych Zwingli did not hold to the Biblical concept of elders, that the elders were responsible for governing the church. Instead, they emphasized the role of the "pastor" as the one governing the church. The reformers used the term "pastor," which is the Latin for "shepherd," to replace the Catholic priest in the minds of their followers So the presiding priest simply became the pastor in charge, again ignoring the elders' position.

The opening lines of John Calvin's *Ecclesiastical Ordinances of 1541* read: "There are four orders or offices instituted by our Lord for the government of his church. First pastors, then doctors, then elders, and fourth deacons."[15] The earliest English versions of the Bible, following Calvin's and Zwingli's leads, translated the original Greek word *poimēn* in Ephesians 4:11, as "pastor," the Latin noun for "shepherd," only compounding the problem.

Today, the words we use as titles continue to perpetuate the confusion. The Greek scholar Daniel B. Wallace asserts that the terms "elder" and "pastor" are not equivalent:

> "Elder" and "pastor" are not the same thing in the New Testament: "Elder" refers to the office one holds by virtue of appointment . . . "Pastor" [shepherding] is a spiritual gift that one is given by the Holy Spirit (cf. Eph. 4:11; 1 Cor. 12:7–11). One can have the gift of "pastor," [that is, shepherding], without being an "elder."[16]

The misuse of these terms, even their interchangeability, concerns many of us. Employing the term "pastor" as a title has gravely harmed many of our congregations' understanding of the role of their elders. And, adopting the titles "Father," "Reverend," or "Pastor" from other polities and ecclesiastical structures has only confused our sheep. We should not use the excuse that "people are used to them." We need to recognize that whenever we deviate from the real meaning of New Testament terminology and employ "pastor" as a title, a great amount of extra-biblical ecclesiastical baggage is already attached. In truth, placing such titles on our leaders has caused us to abandon clear New Testament teaching. It has obscured and diminished the congregation's understanding of the role of elder.

Employing the term "pastor" as a title has gravely harmed many of our congregations' understanding of the role of their elders.

Poimēn, now translated in modern versions either as "pastor" or "shepherd," appears 18 times in the New Testament. In nine instances, it refers to Jesus, where He is called a shepherd. In eight other cases, it refers to a literal shepherd of sheep. *Poimēn* is usually translated "shepherd" in all these places except Ephesians 4:11: "He gave some as apostles, and some as prophets, and some as evangelists, and some as *pastors* and teachers" (italics added). In this case, since the rather incomplete Reformation, we seem to be stuck with this mistranslation of *poimēn*. It should be translated here (as it is everywhere else), as *shepherd*, like it is in the 2016 Text Edition of the ESV.[17] In most other English translations of the New Testament, verse 11 is the only instance in which *poimēn* is translated as "pastor."

The word "pastor" does not occur in the other listings of roles and functions in the New Testament (1 Cor. 12:28, Eph. 4:11–13). Moreover, the New Testament never gives the qualifications for such an office. Regrettably, the use of "pastor" in most translations of Ephesians 4:11 has led to the invalid and unwarranted change from a functional, shepherding description of caring service to an office, title, or position.

The error in using the term "pastor" as the title of an office is compounded when it is used as an honorific title. Jesus specifically forbade this practice:

> "But do not be called Rabbi; for One is your Teacher, and you are all brothers. Do not call anyone on earth your father; for One is your Father, He who is in heaven. Do not be called leaders; for One is your Leader, that is, Christ. But the greatest among you shall be your servant" (Matt. 23:8–11).

In *Biblical Eldership* Alex Strauch points out:

> Of course there were prophets, teachers, apostles, evangelists, leaders, elders, and deacons within the first churches, but these terms were not used as formal titles for individuals. All Christians are saints, but there was no "Saint John." . . . Some are elders, but there was no "Elder Paul."[18]

Over and over, the desire for order, for prominence, or for enforcing orthodoxy led men to create centralized authorities for setting the rules and standards. For centuries, Protestant denominations have retained these extra-biblical traditions and terminology.

As a result, our churches now confront serious and substantial impediments, some inflicted by history, some by our own choices, and a few from ungodly motives. We are having to cope with formidable and deeply ingrained assumptions, practices, and institutions. And we are trying to serve in an increasingly dangerous, secular world that needs our effective presence. How do we deal with this?

Necessary Transformations

If transformation to truly Biblical leadership of our churches is to be accomplished, certain matters must be set right, beginning with the thorough and accurate exposition of Scripture. First, our church's existing, governing body must be convinced by Scripture that plural elder leadership and governance are both Biblical and required. Passive oversight by elected officers or leadership by professional staff are *not* Biblical. They must be replaced, and the changes handled carefully, with large doses of grace, patience, and humility to guide us.

Moreover, these Biblical truths must be carefully explained and taught to our people. Sadly, the essentially theological changes can be easier to achieve than the accompanying cultural changes. The Biblical instruction is so clear and strong, but people are set in their ways and thinking. And, we do not have very many positive examples to emulate or to guide us.

First, our church's existing, governing body must be convinced by Scripture that plural elder leadership and governance are both Biblical and required.

Some prominent men who advocate plural elder rule still continue to carve out preeminent places for themselves as "Senior Pastors," thereby compromising the Biblical teaching on the equality of elders. In their writings John MacArthur, Gene Getz, and Mark Dever strongly advocate church governance by a plurality of elders. However, inconsistent with their Biblical arguments, they still reserve for themselves the position and title of Senior Pastor.[19] To his credit, in 2003 John MacArthur minimized his senior pastor title by saying : "I am just a pastor-teacher named John."[20] However, in his book *Pastoral Ministry* (2005), MacArthur's coauthor Alex Montoya maintained that: "The pastor is the one called to provide leadership for the church, regardless of church polity."[21]

Even if a church decides to have elders, that does not necessarily mean it will institute the *plural Biblical eldership* which meets New Testament standards. Look at the incomplete models around us. Some churches have a single elder, the pastor, or a senior pastor who is in authority over the elders. Others have elders who are handpicked by the pastor, because they agree with him and support his agenda. Other bodies have elders who function like a board of directors. They set policy for the staff who are leading the ministries, but the elders themselves are not personally involved in ministry leadership.

None of these half measures meet the apostles' intent or the New Testament model of shared leadership by elders. Worse, they do not empower the members of Christ's body for His service (Eph. 4:12).

Second, and simultaneously, our fellow believers must be taught to see themselves as Scripture does: They are God's family, chosen for the high calling of service. They are, in fact, His gifted servants (Rom. 12:5–6), designed uniquely for a myriad of tasks, just as are all the diverse components of the human body. This new point of view involves transformation of members' customary attitudes, cultures, and comfort niches. Instead of being considered consumers, or passive observers served by professional staffs, Christians must be seen as a reservoir of God-given gifts, ready to be equipped and enabled to participate in active service (Eph. 2:10), under the leadership of the elders.

Even if a church decides to have elders, that does not necessarily mean it will institute the *plural Biblical eldership* which meets New Testament standards.

This second change, this transformative step, is often very difficult because of a history of the opposite expectations (often fostered by paid church staff). In many cases, such presumptions are built into the traditions and bylaws of denominations and their associations. Transformation at the top is rare but possible.

The third conversion is this: Elder governance must be redefined as active servant service. Contrary to much current thinking, the church cannot be led or directed by an elder council that is modeled after a modern-day corporate board of directors—persons who do not participate in ministry operations, directors who merely decide policies for implementation by a professional staff. This is called the Carver Model; see pages 55–56.[22] Some churches, like Willow Creek Community Church (in Illinois; 25,000 members), are proud of using this model and urge it upon others.[23] However, the history of this church gives us pause.

On April 9, 2018, Bill Hybels, Willow Creek's senior pastor, CEO, and author of *Who You Are When No One's Looking*,[24] resigned because of allegations of misconduct with women. Later, on August 8, 2018, the *New York Times* announced that the lead pastor who had replaced Hybels *and* the entire elder board had resigned because of their history of failing to keep Hybels accountable. Willow Creek's use of the Carver management model and its egalitarian position on allowing women to serve on the elder board had failed to protect the women of that congregation.[25] Elder Missy Rasmussen confessed to the congregation: "We are sorry that we allowed Bill to operate without the kind of accountability that he should have had."[26]

Real elders are active servants, ministry leaders busy in *leading*—that is, in the actual functioning of ministries. They are personally connected in relationships with those they lead, "sheep" who are experiencing their pastoring love and care. A shepherd leads his flock into beneficial pastures; he does not merely point the way. Successful implementation of plural Biblical eldership depends largely on the church's elders fulfilling their calling as active *under-shepherds* of The Good Shepherd.

Here we should consider our own particular churches. Are these components present? Specifically, are our ministries led by the men who comprise the governing body? If not, can our churches be judged as having true and effective Biblical elder leadership? The initial best of intentions, with strong congregational agreement and enthusiasm, may have ignited the desire to institute changes from previous traditions and structures. But maybe some (or all) of the original

OUR CALLING

Biblical eldership, governance, building blocks were not firmly positioned, leading to the incomplete, poorly functioning versions we have on our hands today.

As we want our churches to measure up to God's standards, this has become the issue: What are these essential and critical building blocks of effective, Biblical, elder leadership?

Chapter 1

Develop Leaders for Eldership

S uppose we represent a church that is searching to change. A growing urgency to transition to New Testament-mandated leadership is emerging. How do we proceed? The logical first step is locating potential elders, men who fully meet the New Testament requirements for Biblical elders.

Some of the New Testament qualities of true elders are clearly stipulated in 1 Timothy 3:1–7, and Titus 1:5–9. And usually in a given congregation, a few available men come close to meeting these requirements. However, Scripture is also plain that even more important guidance is accessible—the obvious previous appointment to eldership by the Holy Spirit: "The Holy Spirit has made you overseers, to shepherd the church of God" (Paul exhorting the Ephesian elders in Acts 20:28). But this divine appointment, when present, is only apparent to the body of believers and its elders as such men are observed *serving as shepherd leaders* of its ministries.

Isn't it a shame that the trend toward "Do It Yourself" in home maintenance has *not* carried over into most churches? Instead, the responsibility for the building and supervision of ministries has been solved by "hiring someone." We have acquiesced to the problematic outsourcing of our obligations to lead and shepherd the flock. We have defaulted to paid staff, those so-called "trained professionals." And we have ignored Jesus' warning about the safety of the sheep under the "hired hand" type of leadership (John 10:12–13).

DEVELOP LEADERS FOR ELDERSHIP

Paul saw that it was important that the first churches he planted had the right kind of critically needed leadership. He instructed his coworker Titus: "For this reason I left you in Crete, that you would set in order what remains and appoint elders in every city as I directed you" (Titus 1:5). If the apostles believed that the church's ministries should instead be led by persons it employed, wouldn't they have established the qualifications for, and responsibilities of, such individuals, just as they did for elders and their deacon assistants?

The common trend to hire so-called professionals is not only a substitute for the Biblical instruction to appoint elders, but individual church members who have proven leadership gifts are discouraged from serving. Is it that we cannot risk their involvement since it might diminish the power, control, and supposed efficiency of the professionals? Have we picked up such an attitude from our culture without counting the cost?

"The Holy Spirit has made you overseers, to shepherd the church of God"
—Paul, exhorting the Ephesian elders in Acts 20:28

Often, when a church has a senior pastor, or a "lead pastor," we hear the assertion that "He should have the staff he wants." Translation: He shouldn't have to wait until "laymen" take leadership. Nor should he have to muster the humility and patience to recognize their gifts and work together with them.

If our practice has been to delegate ministry leadership to paid staff, that is all the membership at large will see and no one will voluntarily take up leadership tasks. Unavoidably, these conditions and dispiriting conduct have brought about our present dilemma, a striking shortage of available and willing leadership. As far back as 1999, George Barna pointed out:

> Our research has shown that within the past couple of years the Christian Church has driven away literally more than one million Christians who are gifted leaders. . . . Others left because, in thousands and thousands of churches, a true leader is a threat to the pastor (who, in those cases, is not truly a leader), and is

intentionally kept away from leadership duties. . . . Those [threatened] pastors often assume that the presence of effective lay leaders will inevitably tarnish the pastor's image and job security, placing their livelihood and their platform to do what they enjoy doing (for example, preaching) in jeopardy.[27]

Mark Dever and Jamie Dunlop describe the danger to the body's one-anothering as the result of reliance on hired staff:

With a competent staff in place, a congregation might pass over caring for each other in favor of letting "trained professionals" do the job. Over time, this shift dilutes the depth of commitment a congregation has for one another. . . . [In our] experience, the most common way that church staff undermine community is when they usurp the church's opportunity to build unity through service.[28]

These problems (and attitudes) can only be corrected if the elders direct the church staff to progressively and successfully turn over ministry to volunteers, training them to fill their shoes. Admittedly, redress will be painfully slow, because paid staff may view this as working themselves out of their jobs. But it is Biblical to "equip the saints!"

Missionaries give public testimony of their sacrificial and rewarding service, and the Holy Spirit uses their examples to influence many young people to follow in their steps. Sadly, in contrast, even in most elder-led churches, the elders' efforts are confined to closed-door meetings, invisible to the congregation. The only glimpse of these men's character and quality the church members see is through announcements of their decisions. Consequently, the man in the pew has a distorted picture of the role of an elder. No wonder eldership is often erroneously viewed as a path to title, recognition, and influence, instead of active shepherding and servant leadership. Why would men in most churches aspire to be servant leaders?

Among those concerned about leadership in general there is an ongoing debate as to whether people are born leaders or may be trained to be leaders. A leading expert on leadership, Warren G. Bennis, is of the opinion that:

> The most dangerous leadership myth is that leaders are born—that there is a genetic factor to leadership. This myth asserts that people simply either have certain charismatic qualities or [do] not. That's nonsense; in fact, the opposite is true. Leaders are made rather than born. And the way we become leaders is by learning about leadership through life and job experiences, not with university degrees. [29]

Many good resources on developing elders and instituting Biblical eldership advocate starting with a training course on eldership. This author has contributed to such a program, involving a lengthy study process, supportive mentoring, and supervised exposure to the work of eldership (see page 27). Such preparation is essential and valuable, but we should not assume that it is how elders are produced. It is an appropriate *advanced* step in a prospective elder's development. A prior step is that he has proved himself to have voluntarily followed the Holy Spirit's urging and guidance into hands-on ministry service. There his leadership gifts will be revealed to the elders and those he shepherds. John MacArthur agrees:

> Rather than always devising prefabricated ministry assignments and walking inexperienced young men through every step of what to do, it's sometimes better to give them the freedom to demonstrate what they are made of by seeing how they take up duties that are not necessarily laid at their feet. Then we can give help and encouragement as they develop their own unique spiritual abilities. I find that when men who are gifted and called to leadership are encouraged to think that way, they thrive.[30]

Provide a Path to Eldership

Servant leaders will be (must be) brought to light in the appropriate conducive climate. In such an atmosphere, volunteer service will be the usual expectation, and it will be both sought and honored. The responsibility of the existing governing elders is found in Ephesians

DEVELOP LEADERS FOR ELDERSHIP

4:11–12: They are, as "shepherds and teachers, to equip the saints for *the work of ministry, for building up of the body of Christ*" (ESV).

This equipping by the current responsible leaders will consist in encouraging men in their Christian walk and progressively supervising and mentoring them through various leadership responsibilities of increasing import and scope. Personal, sustained shepherding and training for ministry leadership are indispensable in developing men for true eldership. However, we need to be sure we are encouraging *godly* leadership. We need to be able to recognize those volunteers who are inclined to be *prima donnas*, independent men with inflated egos who can destroy an organization. The church must have men who will build teams, not individual fiefdoms.

Servant leaders will be (must be) brought to light in the appropriate conducive climate.

A huge industry offers leadership training, and those involved naturally emphasize its effectiveness. However, in our experience, and in agreement with Warren Bennis,[31] the most effective training occurs *outside* the classroom, through hands-on efforts. Under the guidance of a mentor, in a climate that encourages initiative, one may develop as a leader. New talent will not emerge unless such conducive and inspiring environments are provided.

The Development of Leadership

Reluctantly, I cite my personal story, but my experiences have shaped my perspective on the development of leadership. Prior to college no one ever said I had any leadership potential. But, after becoming a Christian in my freshman year, I found myself responding to the needs of the student ministry of InterVarsity Christian Fellowship. Some of us saw the need to assume some responsibility for accountability and structure. We had the urgent desire to make a difference. Encouraged by my mentors on IVCF's regional staff, this eventually led to the responsibility of chairing the Baltimore-Washington IVCF chapter for several years. Then I was challenged to obtain more training which led to time out from my career to secure an MDiv from Fuller Theological Seminary in 1959.

Much later, in the mid-1960s, I was hired by General Electric Astro-Space Division as a unit manager. The work was the design of communications payloads for satellites. Soon I discovered that corporate practice for each satellite project was to team with another outside company which was supposed to supply the communications hardware. As a consequence, G.E. repeatedly lost in competitions for contracts because the particular teammate, the communications supplier, did not consider its contribution its highest priority. We did not secure the contracts because our partners did not perform to the degree of excellence required.

Seeing the necessity for an in-house capability for this expertise, and with the support of management, I proceeded to build up a satellite communications unit, from one employee to a subsection of sixty-five engineers, technicians, and several laboratories. That subsection's design efforts became a major factor in G.E.'s 1967 win of the communications satellite contract, Defense Satellite Communications System (DSCS III), in competition with the then preeminent communications satellite suppliers. That contract and its additional follow-ons amounted to two billion dollars in sales.[32]

Personal, sustained shepherding and training for ministry leadership are indispensable in developing men for true eldership.

Another General Electric corporate practice was to send its managers out for cutting-edge leadership training. So, I was sent to both G.E.'s legendary Crotonville management and RCA's program management schools. But I don't think these had much effect on my leadership skills. Instead, I learned to lead on the job, responding to obstacles by inventing and implementing various possible solutions, gradually assembling a talented and diverse team and the required support laboratories. A strong element was that I was favored with mentors and supervisors who provided the freedom to initiate.

While managing this work at G.E. Astro Space Division, I was working hard on another major opportunity to serve the Lord and His people. I was part of a group that stepped up to a need for an evangelical, non-denominational church to serve new believers coming from diverse backgrounds. Many were participating in Bible studies but had no church home. Some were recent converts and others came from widely different theological and cultural backgrounds. The Lord united this group to meet their need for a Biblical, accepting place in which they could be discipled and loved.

That innovative church served many singles, including those recovering from biblically permissible divorces. Many arrived with open issues, and wanting to marry or remarry. My wife and I helped expand an innovative premarital preparation and mentoring program to meet this challenge. Over time more than 500 couples were prepared for godly marriages. The positive outcomes were that 18 percent of the registered couples decided that their marriages would be unwise, and we tracked a 3 percent divorce rate for those who completed the full program.

Here again we used the team approach. We trained a team of seasoned couples with a desire to serve as mentors, one matched to each premarital couple. First, each was mentored through the program themselves as if they were preparing for marriage. Then each couple was assisted in mentoring their first premarital couple. Feedback from these mentors and students showed what was working, or not, and adjustments were made.

This method not only successfully trained mentors but many discovered that, in the conducive supportive environment they could serve the Lord by shepherding others. A significant number of the men found that they were, in fact, servant leaders and the Holy Spirit was calling them to be elders. And other church members and the eldership came to recognize them as the church's elders.

The Most Effective Pathway

Because of these personal experiences, I have very firm opinions on how leadership is developed. The pathway I have found to be most effective begins with the God-given desire to address a need, plus the willingness to shoulder the responsibility and the initiative to simply start. Also, successful leadership in industry or church was never due to just my individual effort. For a leader, cultivating a team is essential. Leaders must be team players I attribute successful leadership to thorough investigation of alternative solutions, and then to the recruitment and nurture of a talented team to implement the chosen solution, and solve the problem or meet the need. Ministry service trains men to employ their leadership gifts and should be the means of finding our potential elders.

James Kouzes and Barry Posner, in *The Leadership Challenge*, point out:

> Challenging opportunities often bring forth skills and abilities that people don't know they have. Given opportunity and support, ordinary men and women can get extraordinary things done in organizations.[33]

Bear in mind that we are not dismissing the appropriate usefulness of a training course for elders, provided it is given at the right time. We can mentor elder candidates, but we cannot create them. Only the Holy Spirit can do that. As an advanced step in equipping such leaders for eldership, the *The Study Guide to Biblical Eldership*, by Alexander Strauch, is a 12-lesson, 24-week inductive and mentoring course.[34] This resource provides the structure for the prospective elder to examine his current role in the church, and the Biblical material on eldership, and to determine how it applies to his own life and in his own church. *The Study Guide* comes with a manual for the facilitator, *The Mentor's Guide to Biblical Eldership*, by Alexander Strauch and this author.[35] It contains the necessary resources and presents the issues to be raised. It has been well received by many who wish to understand and apply the Biblical material to their own situations (53,000 copies in English, plus editions in 14 other languages).

The usual value placed on a man's executive experience as a successful professional in the community may be helpful, or, in fact, it may hinder his work as elder. Even seminary education, while of some help, is no substitute for ministry leadership experience, previously demonstrated within a church body. Some seminaries assume or propagate the senior pastor model of church governance. And some new graduates have not proved they are servant leaders because they have not yet had to be tested in a church or para-church ministry.

Automatically installing as elder the man doing the preaching is another frequent mistake. He may not be qualified for eldership. Servant leadership ability and humility may not accompany his preaching gift. The man's true character can be camouflaged by his successful skill as presenter, his popularity and charisma. Many such men do not have their egos well controlled. Like many of us, they deny their dependence on others.

The high rate of moral failure of so many preachers is seemingly endemic. In national news we are continually reminded of yet another senior pastor of a large church who has had to resign because of a serious moral lapse, behavior involving marital infidelity, sexual abuse, or financial impropriety.

This terrible loss testifies to the significant difficulty godly elders face when they do not encourage and select preaching talent from within the body. When an eldership attempts to make an accurate assessment of a man from outside to fill a vacated pulpit, the responsibility is fraught with danger. They must make an intensive investigation of his behavior and relationships in previous settings. Haven't a good number of moral failures by pastors occurred because the men selected were prominent namely for their preaching ability? What about looking for the certifying evidence that previously they served effectively as equals with other elders? Do they come to us having demonstrated that in the past they benefited from the wisdom and required accountability of peer council elders?

Ministry service trains men to employ their leadership gifts and should be the means of finding our potential elders.

A major reason for the shortage of men qualified for eldership is that leadership service requires a considerable investment in pastoral shepherding: studying, teaching, counseling, leading ministries, training and encouraging volunteers, and tending to the needs of the flock—not to mention those of his own household and family. This is in addition to time spent on meetings, planning, making decisions, and praying. Very often life's accumulated responsibilities preclude such a time commitment. (This may amount to at least ten hours per week, in addition to Sunday duties.) Many of us are not majoring in majors. We are shackled with too much busyness, burdened with too many undertakings. Are we really responsive to Paul's charge?

> I urge you, brethren, by the mercies of God, to present your bodies a living and holy sacrifice, acceptable to God, which is your spiritual service of worship. And do not be conformed to this world, but be transformed by the renewing of your mind, so that you may prove what the will of God is, that which is good and acceptable and perfect (Rom. 12:1–2).

The Scope of Our Ministry

Are we evangelicals too focused on the Sunday morning worship services? The Great Commission challenges us to intentionally identify opportunities to further the gospel, both within the church, but especially beyond. Some internal church activities evangelize our families and friends. However, this is not being fully faithful to Christ's command. However, the truth is that *effective* discipling requires face-to-face, personal interaction, and accountability. Again, Ed Stetzer states:

> We have increasingly seen in churches that are growing through conversion, that they were active, even aggressive, about servicing and engaging in their community. That activity was part of their DNA.[36]

The church cannot act like, or be viewed as, an isolated community, some private club. We must be demonstrating and extending God's redemptive love through our ministries. We can meet real needs while exercising our Christian witness. We must risk the costs of time, effort, patience, and even failure. Ministries that produce the results God intends must reach all age groups and address a multitude of needs, those within and beyond our doors, and out to "all the nations."

If we are to be effective in local evangelistic ministry we must extend our outreach beyond the walls of the church. Our men should be leading in the creation of solutions to problems our communities face. In the process these ministries will surface the leaders the Holy Spirit will tap as true elders.

Have we adequately explored the possibilities for effective evangelism? Many churches discharge our obligation by merely financially supporting overseas mission organizations. But this does not lead to the hands-on involvement of our members. And it does not replicate servants or generate leaders.

There are two types of local outreach ministry for churches. Both are legitimate expressions of Christian love. Examples of the first type are food pantries and thrift shops. These mercy ministries may lead people to have a positive view of the church, but they are not the atmosphere for building relationships.

The other type of outreach offers opportunities for sustained relationships. Some of these ministries can be directly sponsored and staffed by the church. Others provide service and evangelism opportunities for church members, placing them in relationships with people who are unaffiliated with evangelical churches.

If we are to be effective in local evangelistic ministry, we must extend our outreach beyond the walls of the church.

Many churches use Awana, a Bible-based curriculum for children ages 2 through 18, as a way to bring in the unchurched and use the members' gifts to produce disciples and leaders. They help with games and Scripture memory, but the program also incorporates older children mentoring younger children. Though conducted in church facilities, the local community is reached because church families invite their friends. In a program I am familiar with the evening starts with a simple free supper for children and their parents. While the Awana program is underway, parents may attend bible studies or enjoy a date night.

Sponsoring the Boy Scouts used to be an effective means for a church to engage the community. However, its inclusion of LGBT leaders and its history of pedophilia[37] has ruled out association with evangelical churches. A Christian alternative, Trail Life USA, provides a year-round club experience for boys; as of 2017 it had

DEVELOP LEADERS FOR ELDERSHIP

26,000 members. American Heritage Girls, with 43,000 members in 2017, is a Christian alternative to the Girl Scouts. The internet lists over 50 Christian organizations, plus 4-H and equestrian clubs and a myriad of sports clubs, through which churches may extend their witness into their communities. Some of these organizations permit a church to have its own chapter or franchise. This has several advantages. The church may set its own agenda, and the content of programs being offered, while still benefiting from the reputation and the resources of the parent organization. (This is more profitable for the church than individual members' participation in Christian organizations managed by others.)

For adults, effective opportunities address people's needs, and provide for integration of Biblical content and extended relationships:

- Area Bible studies
- MOPS (Mothers of Preschoolers)
- Premarital preparation programs
- Celebrate Recovery (addiction recovery)
- Divorce recovery programs
- Rescue missions programs
- Crisis pregnancy centers
- Legal services societies
- Special needs services
- Neighborhood-based security efforts
- Prison ministries
- Singles ministries
- Programs for refugees and needy ethnic enclaves
- Seniors programs
- Career workshops
- ESL (English as a Second Language) services
- Tutoring
- Hiking clubs
- Weight loss programs
- Native American ministries

Church-sponsored financial and estate counseling also offers an opportunity for ministry, provided these are conducted with this caveat: Those leading the program may not compromise its or the church's integrity by any attempt to market a product or service. This includes the specific promotion of designating the church as the beneficiary of participants' estates.

Many opportunities are available for those who desire to serve Christ in the world, both with the Word and their efforts. Churches searching for such programs for their members should investigate those that already exist in their local areas. Or, members who desire to see the Gospel spread will find the Lord inspiring them to start their own indigenous programs. These initiatives should be viewed as complements to in-house ministries. In all cases, the effectiveness of any ministry and its evangelism depends on godly leadership.

Letting the community know the services the church offers will require publicity. The conventional approach is a billboard in front of the church building promoting such. But this limited exposure applies only to those driving by and may only refer to activities inside the church building. Better to augment this with posters placed in public areas and notices in newspapers and on various types of social media like Nextdoor. Often local newspapers will accept articles describing community services offered by the church.

Many opportunities are available for those who desire to serve Christ in the world, both with the Word and their efforts.

The choice of its name often influences a church's outreach. If the name was chosen to indicate its founders' or its present-day, distinctive theology, it may attract those of the same background moving into the community. However, it may inhibit those who otherwise might be willing to try visiting the church. For the sake of evangelism, a name that suggests an open, loving fellowship is most useful. This is very important to people who are not tied to a certain denomination.

Start with Youth

Unless the church has the culture and practice of encouraging young men (from junior high age on) to serve, they will succumb to worldly pressures to structure their lives around careers, families, sports, and an assortment of choices and obligations which will crowd out the possibility of leading, not to mention eldership. But if elders, church leaders, members, and peers identify and honor leadership gifting in young men, we will be encouraging them to orient their lives around serving the Lord. Discipling, training, and mentoring, with service opportunities of progressive difficulty and responsibility, will prepare young men for eventually assuming significant leadership responsibilities.

For example, one of the most effective opportunities for developing young leaders is the Gap Year program offered by many Christian camps.[38] We are most familiar with the one offered at Camp Elim in Woodland Park, Colorado. High school graduates, with track records of service in their home churches, are offered the opportunity to serve at the camp for one year, prior to entering college or settling on a career.

These young people receive 330 hours of intensive Biblical and leadership training, reinforced by responsible duties with a variety of campers. They are strongly influenced by the intensive mentoring they receive from godly role models. The combination of Biblical studies and service shapes priorities and leads these young believers to make realistic decisions on future plans. Many decide on the lifetime commitment to serve before they turn to the next steps in education or careers.

If elders, church leaders, members, and peers identify and honor leadership gifting in young men, we will be encouraging them to orient their lives around serving the Lord.

Missions trips for young people are invaluable. These can be either to local ethnic populations or other countries. Experiencing another culture and the needs of its people, demonstrating God's love to them through their service and learning to work as a team—all are hands-on preparation for sorting out priorities and being accountable to serve the Lord. Such effort is often the first step in appreciating God's agenda: Christ is "purchas[ing] for God, with [His own] blood, men from every tribe and tongue and people and nation" (Rev. 5:9). And such a commitment of time and energy often opens eyes and commits hearts to further leadership service, even, eventually, Biblical eldership.

An essential benefit of the exposure of servant leadership to the congregation is that these visible examples will inspire younger men to involve themselves in Christian service. Wisdom from the nineteenth-century author Samuel Miller (1769–1850), professor at Princeton Theological Seminary and author of *The Ruling Elder* (1831), is quoted by Mark Dever:

> Wherever you reside, endeavor always to acquire and maintain an influence with young men. They are the hope of the church and of the state; and he who becomes instrumental in imbuing their minds with sentiments of wisdom, virtue, and piety is one of the greatest [of] benefactors. . . They are, therefore, worthy of your special and unwearied attention. . . . In short, employ every Christian method of attaching them to your person and ministry, and of inducing them to take an early interest in the affairs of the church.[39]

To summarize, the true elder is found in the man responsibly serving and leading in the ministries of the church, shepherding the flock. The appointment of such servants as true elders must be preceded by a change in the church's culture. Instead of reliance primarily on paid staff, a fresh commitment must be put into practice—the encouragement and preparation of volunteers from among the believers to be the servant leaders of its ministries. In the effective church, the members desire to serve, and the mindset is to grow leadership. These advancements may take time, but they are necessary before the right men are appointed to eldership and Biblical governance of God's people.

Chapter 2

Appoint Qualified Leaders

Elders must be voluntarily involved in hands-on ministry leadership, that is, "diligently labor[ing]" (1 Thess. 5:12) among us. Therefore, we must recognize and appoint as governing elders only men who are *already serving* as shepherd elders under the prior appointment of the Holy Spirit: "The Holy Spirit has made you overseers" (Acts 20:28). These shepherd leaders are identified by their observable elder qualities and diligent servant service, especially their ministry leadership. We cannot create elders by simple election, or by appointment, or by formal training. The true elder will be singled out because he has been clearly chosen by the Holy Spirit. Gradually this will be understood, and then acknowledged, by the existing eldership, the watching, praying congregation, and the man himself.

Servant leadership is not only demonstrated in an elder's wise, administrative decision-making and his guidance of one or more ministries. He must be actively "holding fast the faithful word which is in accordance with the teaching, so that he will be able both to exhort in sound doctrine and to refute those who contradict" (Titus 1:9). Elder authority is to be exercised primarily through teaching, not through policy decisions and instructions, not by "lording it over those allotted to your charge, but [by] proving to be examples to the flock" (1 Peter 5:3). Like Paul, elders need to be able to say, "I exhort you, be imitators of me" (1 Cor. 4:16); and "You yourselves know, from the first day, . . . how I was with you the whole time, serving the Lord with all humility" (Acts 20:18–19, to the Ephesian elders). Paul supported himself, consistently encouraged and honored his coworkers, and prayed for his fellow brothers and sisters.

We must recognize and appoint as elders only men who are *already serving*, as shepherd elders under the appointment of the Holy Spirit.

All elders must be able to *both* teach and lead, or govern (oversee). There is no Biblical precedence for having two types of elders, "teaching" and "ruling" elders, based on an assumed division of labor, with elders who preach but do not also govern. Moreover, just because a man has the gift of teaching, this by itself does not fit him for eldership. He must be a qualified, ministry, shepherd leader as well. Paul's instruction to Timothy was that the "elders who *rule well* are to be considered worthy of double honor, especially those who work hard at preaching and teaching" (1 Tim. 5:17). Paul requires that we understand that *ruling well* is the greater, over-all category.

Selection of Elders

The choice of the process by which qualified leaders become elders is critical. In many churches the congregation elects their elders, a common practice stemming from our secular, democratic heritage. But the New Testament precedence does not support such election or affirmation: Paul and Barnabas "*appointed* elders . . . in every church" (Acts 14:23, emphasis added).

Often, the precedent for congregational election is claimed from Acts 6:1–7, the choice and then affirmation by the young church of The Seven "to serve tables" (v. 2), that is, to conduct the church's charitable care of its needy. But the choice of those seven men cannot be used as precedence for the election of elders. Those servants' gifts, duties, and authority were quite different from those of the elders. The Seven were chosen to relieve the apostles of a charitable task, a time-consuming effort that was interfering with their significant spiritual priorities, "prayer and . . . the ministry of the word [of God]" (v.4). The Seven were to represent the interests of the different ethnic groups present in the body. Specifically, they were to make sure that their widows were treated fairly in the distribution of benevolent resources. Also, since they were to represent the flock's interests, it was appropriate that The Seven be chosen by those who already knew the reputations of these men. Their duties and the need for this service and were clearly understood by the growing church.

Due to the nature of their gifting and secular experience, many potential elders want to employ the benefits thereof in the church. Others want to "straighten out how the church is run." Worse yet, some men believe eldership offers them status and control. It is certainly true that elders have the God-given authority to exercise oversight of the church body and to make collective decisions for it. But eldership is all about servant leadership, not titles, recognition, and power.

The record of the New Testament does not support the position that the church of today should be governed like a representative democracy. The apostles selected and appointed the first elders. There is absolutely no indication in the New Testament or in the Post-Apostolic writings that this procedure was later changed to election of its officers by the church. The instructions on elder qualifications were given to Timothy and Titus, *not* to congregations.

The record of the New Testament does not support the position that the church of today should be governed like a representative democracy.

The testimony of the Post-Apostolic Fathers does not add any detail, because they wrote little about who did the selecting following the apostles—that is, until the church became hierarchical and the bishops did all the appointing. However, the second century church father Clement wrote of elders being appointed and then approved by the congregation.[40] If the church body simply *approved* of the choices, then it is clear that its existing leaders (elders) had made the appointments beforehand.

APPOINT QUALIFIED LEADERS

The decisive question is this: Who do the elders represent? They are not elected representatives of God's people. They are under-shepherds of Christ, the Chief Shepherd of the Church. It is His church, not the congregation's: "The church of God which He [Christ] purchased with His own blood" (Acts 20:28). The elders are Christ's stewards, entrusted with the care of His church, those who are responsible for shepherding His flock righteously and well, "as those who will give an account" (Heb. 13:17).

Since it is Christ's church, not the congregation's, who is best qualified to search for and determine the mind of Christ, His chosen Biblical elders or the general congregation? The men selected to be elders should be those who have been recognized by the other elders as appointed by the Holy Spirit: "The Holy Spirit has made you overseers, to shepherd the church of God" (Acts 20:28).

The Congregation's Role

Other reasons why election by popular congregational vote is not Biblical or judicious should be given serious consideration.

- As we stated in *Eldership in Action*: "The individual congregant (who is not an elder) cannot be expected to pass authoritative judgment on whether the qualifications of the particular man under consideration are sufficient—that is, whether he meets the high standards set forth in Scripture. Requiring the church membership to make this evaluation is equivalent to asking the community of a medical specialist's patients to certify his credentials, instead of insisting that he be board-certified by his peers."[41] Surgeons are board-certified by surgeons, not by the general public. Lawyers are admitted to the bar by other lawyers, not by the local populace, or by their clients.

- Evaluating a candidate's qualifications for eldership requires assembling the pertinent information. What are his priorities? What service and shepherding is the man giving the body? Because much of his effort may have been away from public

37

view, or in a specific ministry, most of the congregation may not be aware of it. Only the present elders who have been mentoring the candidate are qualified to appoint him: "Do not lay hands upon anyone too hastily and thereby share responsibility for the sins of others; keep yourself free from sin" (1 Tim. 5:22).

- The decision as to a candidate's qualifications should be preceded by a thoughtful discussion of all the evidence involved. A congregational meeting for voting does not provide such an opportunity. Moreover, the individual, voting church member is not ever held accountable for congregational decisions. He does not have to explain the rationale for its choices or his. Scripture teaches that it is not the flock, but the *elders* "who will [be required to] give an account" (Heb. 13:17).

- One consequence of congregational ratification is the probability of control by a small minority. In a church with a 25 percent quorum requirement (in order to conduct business at the all-church meeting), a matter can be decided by as little as 13 percent of the members. The situation is even worse in the case of a two-thirds vote for ratification. Then a mere 9 percent of the 25 percent present can prevent a man from serving as elder.

- The church that institutes congregational voting to elect its elder council is putting women in the unbiblical position of exercising authority over men: "But I do not allow a woman to teach or exercise authority over a man" (Paul to Timothy, 1 Tim. 2:12). Such a practice makes the church responsible (through its bylaws) for requiring women to be in authority over men and to take action forbidden in Scripture. No greater exercise of authority than that involved in appointment of elders is presented to a congregation.

Bear in mind that a man should never be appointed to eldership primarily because he represents or supports a certain faction within the leadership. This is completely different from the advice coming from some senior pastors. They advise their compatriots to involve themselves in the elder selection process in order to achieve a governing council that will support their particular philosophies of ministry.[42] But the standards of elder equality and plurality make it absolutely necessary that the church be governed by a group of men whose primary loyalty is to Christ and His teachings. They are His under-shepherds. They may not be beholden to any other leader or be influenced by previous experience in any other polity.

- The congregation does have an important responsibility, crucial for the best governance of God's people. Before the actual appointment of any new elder, the current elders should give the body opportunities to bring to their attention any facts supporting his selection, or proving that the man is not qualified. The elders should solicit the church members' comments, and commit to investigate and determine the truth of any opinion or evidence so offered. This guarantees that the council's decision, either to affirm or quietly disqualify the man, is based on all available, accurate information.

- This form of participation in the elder appointment process actually empowers the individual church member. In the congregational meeting his or her influence is one vote, or involvement in a hazardous, public debate on the qualifications of a potential elder. Instead, by earlier and privately bringing information to the council while it is considering a candidate, the individual congregant may be assured that the council will carefully investigate his testimony, and he may well have a major effect on the outcome. Also, any woman may legitimately bring a concern about, or an affirmation of, a prospective elder to the council for their investigation. Ultimately, the congregation affirms or disapproves the composition of the elder council through its attendance, participation in ministries, and financial giving.

What do we do in the instance of a new church plant, or if the church is just starting to have elders, and there are no existing elders to make the appointments to its governing council? Such a church should seek the advice and counsel of the eldership of another body, one that practices Biblical eldership, to assist in the examination and appointment of its own elders. This wise course of seeking advice and guidance is thoroughly Biblical: "Without counsel plans fail, but with many advisors they succeed" (Prov. 15:22).

In addition to his individual ministry leadership and service in many roles, the Biblical elder partakes in the corporate decisions of the elder council. So, then how does he contribute to the council's making godly and effective decisions?

Chapter 3

Effective Leadership

In addition to his personal leadership in a church ministry, each elder is serving on the elder council, working as a team. The council's primary collective tasks, as distinguished from the ministry leadership duties of each man, are the effective oversight of the current life of the body and preparation for its future. The congregation must be governed by a team of true shepherd elders, each working in one or more areas or ministries. Their efforts, through the hard work of gaining consensus, should determine and implement for the church all decisions on priorities, policies, financial matters, and vision-casting, including the content of the teaching and preaching. As George Barna cautions: "A team without goals and plans is merely a social club."[43]

The council's primary collective tasks . . . are the effective oversight of the current life of the body and preparation for its future.

The fact that such servant elders are ministry leaders gives them the hands-on experience necessary for making wise decisions for the whole church. Their personal contact and demonstrated love for its individual members will undergird the decisions of the elder council with credibility. The elders must see that *all* the needs of their people are addressed, either directly by individual council members and their deacon assistants,[44] or through the structures and ministries the council puts in place and continues to oversee.

The Right Size Council

To be effective, the elder council must make decisions that are timely, will meet the needs of the church, and will be supported by its members. So, to successfully shoulder these responsibilities, how large should the elder council be? It is so easy to neutralize the advantages and productivity of elder governance with an elder council of the wrong size.

The New Testament does not settle the question. Aside from requiring a plurality of (that is, several) elders, nothing about the size of the governing elder council has been provided. The only evidence given is from Paul and Barnabas who "appointed elders [note the plural] for them [the believers] in every church" (Acts 14:23). Paul directed church planter Timothy as to the elder's qualities and duties (1 Tim. 3), but wrote nothing about the number to be appointed. Even Peter, as their "fellow elder," merely "exhort[ed] the elders . . . [to] shepherd the flock of God, . . . exercising oversight" (1 Peter 5:1–2). Not a word about how many or how the men were to function, other than as humble examples to the flock (v. 3). But we may glean some wisdom from the good results we now see in those present-day churches that are successfully doing the work of glorifying the Lord and growing disciples.

To be effective, the elder council must make decisions that are timely, will meet the needs of the church, and will be supported by its members.

The elder council must not be so small that it is controlled by one person, or that it becomes an elite group that violates the principle that governing is to be by a *plurality* of elders, men who are equal in authority and sufficiently diverse to assure independent thinking. One example of an elite group is the council composed of a small number who were chosen by their pastor because of their loyalty to him, rather than for their authentic elder qualities and ministry leadership. Another instance is the council consisting only of paid staff serving under the supervision of a senior or executive pastor and dependent on him for their continued employment.

A council must be large enough to assure that its decisions are the result of thoughtful discussion by men who have prayerfully and independently considered the wisdom of any given course of action. Therefore, the under-shepherd who leads a small church, or desires to plant one with Biblical governance, must avoid solo leadership. Rather, right from the outset, he must establish peer relationships with other men who will share in elder leadership and ministries. "Without consultation, plans are frustrated, but with many counselors they succeed" (Prov. 15:22); "The way of a fool is right in his own eyes, but a wise man is he who listens to counsel" (Prov. 12:15). Once the troops have been led down the wrong course, turning them around is very hard.

A council must be large enough to assure that its decisions are the result of thoughtful discussion by men who have prayerfully and independently considered the wisdom of any given course of action.

However, we can err in the opposite direction, and destroy our council's effectiveness with one that is too large. The senior pastor of a mega-church with thousands of members once told me that, like Moses, he had 70 elders who met only four times a year. Puzzled, I asked what he called this form of governance. With a big grin, he answered, "Benevolent dictatorship!" Moses appointed 70 elders to govern a nation, not a church.

Exchange of opinions and perspectives and focused prayer are all required in godly leading, but there are practical limits on the number of elders involved in the council's decision-making. Management experts hold that a decision-making group should not have more than seven members (eight allows for one to be absent). Even lesser number for an effective group is suggested by George Barna:

A large group cannot lead. Anyone who has been involved in effective leadership knows that once a team gets beyond six people, it becomes unwieldy and degenerates into compromises that reflect the lowest common denominator. At that stage, the focus of the group is not upon a commonly held vision but upon producing some tangible outcome with which everyone is comfortable. That is not leadership; it is accommodation. Effective leadership teams typically have three to five people. Less than three leaves you without the horsepower to get the job done. More than five produces inefficiencies and excessive compromise.[45]

Secular experience is pertinent here. Michael Doyle and David Straus agree that, regardless of venue, when a group exceeds seven, informed and timely discussion of complex issues is impossible.[46] And a management study at Harvard Business School has shown that the optimal size of a group for decision-making is seven, with a 10 percent decrease in efficiency with the addition of another member.[47] These findings of the Harvard Study are no surprise for many reasons, and have been routinely experienced by most leaders. Stephen Robbins sums up the conclusions of many studies on organizational behavior:

> Large groups—with a dozen or more members—are good for gaining diverse input. So, if the goal of the group is fact-finding, larger groups should be more effective. On the other hand, smaller groups are better at doing something productive with that input. Groups of approximately seven members, therefore, tend to be more effective for taking action.[48]

Reasons a large council cannot effectively lead:

- Too many men on the council limit debate. Productive debate requires the back-and-forth clarification of an issue by *all* speakers involved. Adequate participation in give-and-take discussion and multiple inputs from all members are impossible with groups of over seven. As a result, participants are denied the opportunity to employ their gifts and learn from each other. They are not really able to shepherd the flock.

- The time involved in the deliberation needed to achieve a consensus decision is directly proportional to the number of men involved. Most of the elders of a large council will remain passive, while only a few participate in the deliberation. Simply asking each elder for his opinion before voting is not deliberation. Because of the press of time, an alternative, negative outcome is often the result. Therefore, when a council exceeds the optimum size limit, it can no longer effectively work out solutions for the church's issues.

- In large meetings the contributions of the first persons to speak are often forgotten and lost as the discussion progresses prior to a decision being made. As a result, decisions are not based on the *combined* Biblical insight of the participants.

- By necessity, decisions made in meetings of more than seven are achieved by voting rather than by consensus. Voting produces winners and losers; it may later lead to only half-hearted support of an action or policy by some of the elders, or even to divisions in the congregation.

- Consequently, and sadly, as its size grows beyond seven, an elder council degenerates into a passive board of directors, usually mere confirmers of the work of a professional staff.

From my own experience, this observation: A meeting of five to seven men has proved to be highly productive. Its uninhibited personal exchange is much more profitable than the necessarily constricted discussion in the formal meeting of a larger number. I base this conclusion on years of chairing larger groups (at times, a very unproductive and painful experience), and on the review of many studies on the dynamics of deliberative groups.

However, two factors should be understood before we arbitrarily restrict the total number of elders on the council. First, Scripture states that men should aspire to eldership (1 Tim. 3:1), and that they are appointed by the Holy Spirit (Acts 20:28). Second, the number of council elders should be established by how many qualified men the

Lord calls to be elders, *never* by the size of the church. The preferred means of providing a church with its total component of elders is this: All those who aspire to eldership, are biblically qualified, and show evidence of their appointment by the Holy Spirit—as they are seen serving as leaders by the present eldership and the congregation—should be formally recognized.

Delegation to an Executive Team

In a large council the overall quality of elder leadership is diminished. Such a group cannot effectively or efficiently manage the dynamic life of a growing church. The solution is delegation of day-to-day operations, guidance, and coordination of its ministries to an executive team composed of some of the council's number.

All true elders in the church body, those appointed by the Holy Spirit, should be recognized. However, if there is a large number, the total component of elders should select seven or eight to serve as that delegated management team. The other council elders will continue to contribute, according to their gifts, such as teaching and counseling. Other assistance is available from the deacons, whose role is to assist the elders. By these means God's people will be well-led and cared for by its shepherds.

In a large council the overall quality of elder leadership is diminished. Such a group cannot effectively or efficiently manage the dynamic life of a growing church.

One stipulation: Those elders not on the executive team still retain their Biblical governing authority and accountability. No Biblical or logical precedence holds that the true elder does not participate in governing or have leadership responsibilities. By definition, he is accountable for sharing in these. However, there must be a division of labor in order to cover the congregation's needs and outreach efforts.

The major body of elders in the church—the council—must be fully informed of the work of the delegated executive team. The full council must approve anything that could affect the direction of church ministries. At the same time, the council must hold the executive team accountable for execution of all directions the full council has previously approved, and for the coordination of the ministries it has chartered.

Elders must not default decisions to staff simply because the council does not meet often enough to respond to all the needs of the church. Doing so leads to dual (and dueling) lines of authority, and church members and ministry leaders will not really understand who is leading whom. Normally and necessarily in a staff-run entity, its leadership meets at least once a week. Likewise, in an elder-led church an equal commitment by the tent-making elders on its council or its leadership team is needed. This is in addition to each elder's fulfilling his individual ministry leadership responsibilities.

Elders must not default decisions to staff simply because the council does not meet often enough to respond to all the needs of the church.

Many will say that this commitment is asking too much of a man who is not a vocational elder, that is, on staff or paid. Indeed, this will be too much for a man who misunderstands Biblical eldership, or who serves on a council that functions like a secular board of directors. However, the true elder—the man who has been called by the Holy Spirit to serve in ministry leadership—will be willing to commit to such an effort and to shoulder such responsibility. Whether he also will be supported in this by his wife and family is a critical question.

Consensus Council Decisions

A fundamental issue is: How can we elders, using our varied gifts and experience, make good decisions and so honorably lead and oversee Christ's people? Hardly anything is more disastrous for the church body than significant division in its elder council. Any decision reached by only a majority of the elders leaves the council divided and hampered in its leadership. Also, hiding such a split decision from the congregation almost never works. Once the situation is revealed, by the lack of support on the part of some of the elders, or worse, by being leaked and causing gossip, dissention results. Council decisions must be achieved by consensus. This standard of consensus unites the council and permits each elder to wholeheartedly promote implementation. Therefore, if consensus cannot be reached, decisions should be deferred. No elder should be pressured into agreement for the sake of unanimity. However, a pressing crisis may require implementation of a majority decision.

Being unified on an issue or policy means that, after thorough and timely debate, discussion, and prayer, *all* the elders of the council agree to support that particular collective decision which is deemed the best possible choice. It will be that certain choice made only after the well-being of the church and the concerns of *all* the elders have been considered.

Council decisions must be achieved by consensus. This standard of consensus unites the council and permits each elder to wholeheartedly promote implementation.

Consensus decision-making does not mean that every choice will be one that each council member would have preferred. Because we have different histories, gifts, and personalities, unity requires the hard work of applying Christian virtues, namely: "Be devoted to one another in brotherly love; give preference to one another in honor" (Rom. 12:10). Biblically, unity depends on humility (Eph. 4:1–3; Phil. 2:1–5). Making council decisions is an active exercise in corporate (that is, of the entire group), or collegiate (collectively considered by individuals), decision-making. No individual elder has the right to insist that the outcome be based on his own opinion. He must contribute the benefits of his own gifts to a wise decision reached by the whole elder council. And the other brothers must *honor* the differing gifts the Holy Spirit has authored. No doubt, this often requires painstaking, difficult work.

However, two potential complications have proved that making unanimity a requirement (especially in councils with a good number of men), is not wise. First, this practice of asserting unanimity as essential fails to safeguard the church against threats. The worst would be the "savage wolves," predicted in Acts 20:29, arising from within the elders' ranks.

The threat may not look serious or be that blatant. It may be just one strongly opinionated or biased elder who is able to shut down the council's decision-making process. The man may appear quietly cautious, but, in truth, be selfish and obstinately obstructionist. So, the choice to require unanimous consent on all decisions can also be the decision to allow any individual elder to block the council from taking action to protect God's people. Even if we are very careful in appointing elders, the risk remains that one or more may prove to be motivated by self-interest or a strong, narrow theological position. Unanimity is a goal to be sought, but legislating it may convert the goal of unity of the whole into the tyranny of an individual. Not taking an action is as much a decision as taking an action. Granting one council member the privilege of stopping progress violates the absolute requirement that all decisions are to be made by a *plurality* of elders.

Making council decisions is an active exercise in corporate (that is, of the entire group), or collegiate (collectively considered by individuals), decision-making.

In those issues, in which unanimity is extremely difficult, breakdown in the council's protection of the congregation can occur. The stories each of us could tell are disturbing and heartbreaking. For instance, shockingly, so many churches in the United States have experienced the unexpected moral failure of a leader. Such leaders have usually built close relationships with some of the church's elders. When a crisis caused by the guilty party's failure occurs, the leadership may handle matters poorly, responding with silence or denial. The man's close friends on the council often are unwittingly willing to jeopardize the safety and the purity of the church in the desire to show mercy to their friend. The inability to deal biblically with a fallen leader has destroyed many churches. And there seems to be no end to these disturbing emergencies.

Secondly, the elder council that requires unanimity for its decisions will often deadlock. And this can happen over issues of far less consequence than that of "a wolf." A single elder may disagree with a certain idea or plan and the council is obstructed. Perhaps something from his past personal history dominates his thinking. His point of view should be given serious consideration. However, the council is responsible for the protection and ongoing health of the flock. Avoiding acceptance of the idiosyncratic position of one its members—for example, a bias in favor of the status quo—prevents harm, especially when the church's challenges are ever-changing.

Granting one council member the privilege of stopping progress violates the absolute requirement that all decisions are to be made by a *plurality* of elders.

The common practice of requiring the approval of only a majority to decide a matter is also highly destructive. The council that achieves a decision only through a majority vote is divided and unable to lead. A proposal that does not gain the concurrence of all (or nearly all), the elders is not worthy of their support. Elders must be united if they expect the congregation to follow their lead.

Elders willing to make courageous decisions will really lead, not merely manage. Attaining consensus as to Christ's best for the church requires concerted effort. If we just settle on the lowest common denominator to achieve decisions, we are not fulfilling our duty to the Head of the Church. The gold standard for eldership decisions is that they be based on full study of sufficient accurate information and prayer. Such godly effort will be favored with the greatest prospects and support.

First Among Equals?

The phrase first among equals, or *primi inter pares*, often comes up in any discussion of church governance. It was originally applied to the Roman Emperors. The *accurate* application of first among equals is that certain elders in a council of equals will distinguish themselves—by virtue of their gifts, abilities, and God's calling—in providing direction of certain efforts and for limited periods.

The church must have strong, effective leadership initiating, organizing, and providing oversight of its ministries. But an entire council may find it hard to organize a new ministry or program. So, at the outset, some one elder probably will formulate such a proposed effort. The same is true for all other aspects of the council's leadership. It will be expressed through individual elders taking the lead on a variety of occasions and projects, as the council delegates responsibility to the appropriately gifted individuals in their midst.

At times one particular elder's input on a certain aspect of ministry deserves exceptional consideration. Based on his gifting, personal leading of a certain ministry, and extensive experience in that aspect, he is first among equals. This selective leadership and responsibility should be temporary and in terms of the body's specific need.

The principle of first among equals asserts responsible Biblical leadership, leadership which is derived from calling and gifting. It does *not* allow the exercise of power over others because of a select office, position, or title (assumed or officially bestowed). The concept of first among equals is perverted when used to justify a permanent, preeminent position for an individual. Elevating one man to be in charge of all aspects of the church also defies the principle of responsible Biblical leadership. This improper application denies the body the servant leadership of others who may be more gifted to lead under certain current or future circumstances. But this perversion is not always entirely the fault of the one claiming to be first among equals. Often churches and their governing boards will seek a "king," or endow their preachers with priestly status (1 Sam. 8:4–9).

The principle of first among equals asserts responsible Biblical leadership, leadership which is derived from calling and gifting.

When an elder serves in a temporary, first among equals role, it is essential that the other elders, not he himself, have placed him in that role, based on their assessment that he is the best person to address a certain ministry need and at that time (for instance, management of a capital campaign). First among equals is destructive when it is determined by an individual for his own benefit. Jesus taught His disciples:

> "You know that the rulers of the Gentiles lord it over them, and their great men exercise authority over them. It is not this way among you, but whoever wishes to become great among you shall be your servant, and whoever wishes to be first among you shall be your slave; just as the Son of Man did not come to be served, but to serve, and to give His life a ransom for many" (Matt. 20:25–28).

I put this question of who is in charge in a large church to one of its elders. He answered properly and wisely, "That depends on the subject under consideration."

Far too often these days the concept of first among equals is not applied biblically. Many are using it to nullify the principle of equality of elders, and to justify an unbiblical leadership role, usually titled "senior pastor," or "lead pastor." Here the same individual continually occupies a certain leadership position, or is the supposed head or leader of everything in the entire church, regardless of gifting, his or that of others. As Alex Strauch points out, even though Peter, Paul, and James were at times first among equals, they were never senior pastors, and the other apostles never composed their staffs.[49]

Therefore, there must be no hierarchy within the council or permanent first among equals. John Murray, one of the founders of Westminster Theological Seminary in 1929, held that:

> The principal of parity is co-ordinate with that of plurality. Strictly speaking, there can be no plurality if there is not parity. For if one is in the least degree above the others, then in respect to that hegemony, there is no longer plurality.[50]

First among equals can be a very dangerous assertion unless the role is limited in scope and duration. The legitimate application of first among equals must always be free of the expectation or assumption of a position of power over the other elders. And it must always be according to definitive, prescribed current circumstances.

Groupthink Prevention

Responsible leadership involves sometimes saying "wait," or even "no." Many leaders, including this author, regret participating in group decisions that seemed so right at the time, but, when given more thought, tested by time, or evaluated by impartial observers proved to be very flawed. A major cause of such leadership failures is what is called *groupthink*, defined as:

> A psychological phenomenon that occurs within a group of people, in which the desire for harmony or conformity in the group results in an irrational or dysfunctional decision-making outcome. Group members try to minimize conflict and reach a consensus decision without critical evaluation of alternative viewpoints, by actively suppressing dissenting viewpoints, and by isolating themselves from outside influences.[51]

A council may be swayed by an enthusiastic presentation of the proposed benefits of a certain decision, or the argument for immediate action. What may be neglected in the moment is careful consideration of the decision's downsides. Leaders do not like to be viewed as obstructionists. The elder who points out potential negative outcomes may be viewed as having an oppositional attitude, a stance to which all of us are averse. But constructive criticism is not divisive. Elders are responsible for raising any questions about proposed decisions. The freedom to articulate such input should be encouraged.

Groupthink can also be caused by overlooking or ignoring certain unintended consequences. Sometimes the concerns of some affected individuals are not considered at the outset. The absence of thorough consideration and debate on alternatives results in careless actions. Our prayers before making decisions must include requests for wisdom and for the awareness of all the ramifications for, and needs of, all the people involved. Our most godly leadership skills must be brought to bear. Failure to seek affirming guidance from the Lord will lead to harm and hurt. It may even provoke division, in the council or in the church.

Chapter 4

Aspects of Elder Leadership

Management

You have probably noticed that, in referring to elder oversight, I do not use the term *board*, as in "Board of Elders." It is not found in Scripture, has secular connotations, and should be avoided. The adoption of the corporate board model for church governance and structures has been highly destructive. There are very significant differences between a Biblical elder council and any corporate board of directors seen in business enterprises (see page 57).

Further, many churches conduct their efforts through separate boards, of elders and trustees. This is a serious mistake. The ministry priorities of any church are invariably expressed through its leadership's financial preferences and choices. Finances are clearly a spiritual matter: "'For where your treasure is, there your heart will be also'" (Matt. 6:21). Managing the church's finances and fiscal policies is clearly the elders' leadership responsibility.

Dual boards of elders and trustees usually cause just that, dueling—division and dissention—because the two boards have competing agendas and authority. In such an arrangement, the elders will prioritize ministries and vision, presenting the Word and evangelism. The trustees' priority will be the best (in their opinion) use of, and especially conservation of, resources.

In faithful leading, the same responsible leaders must address both spiritual and pragmatic considerations in order to reach quality, God-honoring decisions. Therefore, financial decisions must be made by the elders. Once confident their conclusions align with the Lord's will and the church's mission, the elders must express their leadership in financial matters openly by explaining their decisions to the body while asking for its support.

In faithful leading, the same responsible leaders must address both spiritual and pragmatic considerations in order to reach quality, God-honoring decisions.

Decisions to support both current and future ministries must be based upon prayerful, prudent deliberation, and then any resulting or anticipated financial challenges brought to the congregation. Limiting future ministry initiatives to funds currently available amounts to lack of foresight and faith. Without violating this aspect of the elders' management responsibility, and under their direction, a non-elder may act as church treasurer, or a committee of financial advisers may assist the elders. If state incorporation laws require that the church have a board of trustees, the elder council may designate itself as such.

Structure

Many churches have fallen into, or have been led into, the trap of adopting the very popular Carver Theory of Policy Governance.[52] Originally designed to be used in secular and non-profit corporate environments, it delineates the functioning of corporate boards. When applied to a church, the Carver model of governance has the church's elder council serve as directors, individuals responsible to set policy to be implemented by a staff. Under this structure all operations and ministry leadership are delegated to the professionals, with such a staff headed by a CEO. But biblically, unlike in a secular corporation, the church's functions, its *operations*—that is, its ministries—are the elders' responsibility.

The Carvers advise that a board of directors focus on setting policies. Then, in this context, the church's CEO and staff are chartered to make all ministry management decisions. Today many a senior pastor has appropriated this Carver management structure and positioned himself as the church's CEO. This title defines his oversight and appears to enhance his status. It is especially favored by the man who wants to retain personal control and to manage all church operations through his staff.

The Carver management approach is both biblically unacceptable and tragic for the church. Boards of directors are required for both for-profit and non-profit organizations which have owners—the stockholders in the case of a for-profit organization, or donors in the case of a non-profit organization. The organization's paid staff cannot be trusted to represent the interests of these owners. Those staff managers must be supervised by an independent board of directors whose job it is to establish management's performance standards and salaries.

Contrast the above structure to that in an entity owned by the managers themselves. In that case, a board of directors is not needed; for example, in a family business the owners are the managers. Similarly, a law firm's affairs are directed by its senior partners, its owners. A Biblical church will have this very management structure of ownership and responsibility because, as God's under-shepherds or stewards, the elders collectively function on behalf of the Owner, Christ.

The Carver management approach is both biblically unacceptable and tragic for the church.

In a church with Biblical eldership, its elder council cannot fulfill its leadership responsibilities through mere delegation of management of the church's ministries to employees. It cannot serve as a corporate board of directors. There are fundamental differences between the two governing leadership structures.[53]

ASPECTS OF ELDER LEADERSHIP

BIBLICAL ELDER COUNCIL

The council is accountable to, and represents God, the Owner, and is not responsible to the congregation.

The elders manage as active leaders and under-shepherds.

Each elder on the council is an actual ministry leader or key participant. He manages from a base of direct experience in the body, with its people.

The council directs any necessary paid staff to perform designated duties (church operations).

The church does not have a CEO because all its elders are equal in authority.

Salaried elders, together with tent-making elders, hold one another mutually accountable for their leadership, and for the health of the body.

BOARD OF DIRECTORS

The board serves, and is responsible to, the owners— the stockholders or donors.

The individual directors are passive (not hands-on) managers.

The individual directors have no actual involvement in the entity's daily operations. They must act on information supplied by the CEO.

The board of directors carries out all operations through its essential paid staff.

The board of directors elects a CEO who is then accountable only to that board.

Corporate staffs are rewarded (or not) through salary increases and bonuses, based on meeting standards set by the board's directors.

The experience and first-hand knowledge gained from voluntarily and personally leading specific ministries, and from the accompanying close working relationships with those serving in those ministries, are essential for the elders. They must have this foundation as collectively, as the council, they make decisions for the church, and for which they will have to give an account to the Lord (Heb. 13:17).

Staff

At times an essential skill cannot be found in a volunteer, or full-time service by a particular individual (or in a certain area), is needed. In those cases, it may be necessary to employ someone. However, this move is potentially dangerous. The decision to hire staff proves wise only if the percentage of church members personally involved in ministry *increases* as a result. Moreover, the employee must be tasked to be a trainer and facilitator of volunteers. In his book on ministry teams, T. J. Addington states:

> One of the greatest dysfunctions of the church today is that of "professional ministry" where we hire experts to do ministry rather than equip the body of Christ to do it.[54]

A tipping point away from Biblical elder governance occurs when significant ministry leadership comes from employees. The danger is greatly magnified when paid staff reports to an administrator or pastor instead of to the elder council. John Piper observes:

> Professionalism has nothing to do with the essence and heart of the Christian ministry. The more professional we long to be, the more spiritual death we will leave in our wake.[55]

Some pastors prefer so-called "professional" staff to volunteers. Under such a structure, a pastor can tell his staff what to do and how to do it, and, as their employer, hold them accountable. On the other hand, volunteers require patience, forbearance, and time-consuming encouragement and shepherding. Often it is argued that several volunteers are needed to perform the work of one full-time employee. But this should be considered a positive factor since more members become involved and experience the benefit of sharing in serving.

Many newly planted churches start out well, with active participation in leadership by the founding members. But, with growth and staff replacing the founders, such leadership becomes seriously compromised. Adding staff can be the greatest threat to the active participation in ministry of the members of the congregation. Paid staff should not do the work that member volunteers could and should do. Dependence upon staff often creates a consumer mentality.

The decision to hire staff proves wise only if the percentage of church members personally involved in ministry *increases* as a result.

Under Mike Slaughter, the Ginghamsburg Church in Ohio grew from 100 to 5000 attenders over four decades by means of replication through discipling. The church operates nineteen separate evangelistic community service ministries within the Dayton area. While well-acquainted with salaried staff because of the size of the Ginghamsburg Church, Slaughter explains the downside of using them instead of discipled volunteers:

> Growth provides the fiscal resources to increase professional staff and programing. The experience of mission that was once the task of an unpaid servant is now assigned to a paid staff person. Unpaid servants are assigned the passive work of committees while paid staff performs the active role of mission.
>
> The unintended consequence is the shift from the experiential model, where one learns by doing, to the academy model, where one learns by study. Discipleship occurs in the active process of doing. We err when we try to create transformation in people's lives through the transference of concepts rather than through participation in mission. The Disciples learned as they traveled and ministered with Jesus. We fail to make disciples when we reduce the meaning of discipleship to the assimilation of ideas.[56]

ASPECTS OF ELDER LEADERSHIP

A church should never resemble that affluent club where all the needs of its members are met by the employees. Christians grow most rapidly when they are busy in meaningful service and experience the Holy Spirit working through them. We should not rob our brothers and sisters of such opportunities. When it is absolutely necessary to hire staff, the damage to member involvement can be minimized. The employee's job will be to facilitate ministry by the church members instead of conducting ministry himself.[57] And any such employee should report to the elder council, not to an executive or senior pastor. This avoids the confusion and potential conflict arising from several lines of authority.

**Adding staff can be the greatest threat to
the active participation in ministry of the
members of the congregation.**

Though I prefer "equipped saints" to his use of the term "laity," George Barna's research adds evidence to support this method of meeting the congregation's needs through the leadership skills and service of its volunteers:

> One of the most impressive—and important—elements of leadership in the highly effective churches is that most of the leadership comes from the laity. Analysts often focus on the abilities of the pastor, but we find that every highly effective church is able to exploit opportunities and overcome obstacles because of the depth of its lay leadership.[58]

The principle should always be that we grow our own. Any required volunteer or paid staff should come from within the body if possible. Such a person is much more likely to have embraced the congregation's established values. A good example is the case in which the church needs a youth leader to manage a growing high school group. Best to choose a young fellow from a church family who has already experienced the elders' expectations. Another instance is seen in the necessity for a director of counseling services. If such a trained professional could be found in someone who grew up in the church's culture, he or she would be a wise choice. All of us should always be watching for, and encouraging, the emerging talent God is growing in, or bringing to, our midst.

Preaching and Teaching

The elders' responsible authority and oversight cannot and should not be revealed to the congregation primarily through public announcements of the council's decisions and directions. That is needed, but a Biblical eldership will demonstrate its responsible leadership through expository teaching. The members' understanding of the church's distinctive practices—and the testimonies of their everyday lives—should be based on the natural application of the Scripture passages being taught. How the church worships, how it is governed, and the witness of its members must reflect Scripture's standards. The willingness and ability to teach are required in the true elder.

> He will be able both to exhort in sound doctrine and to refute those who contradict (Titus 1:9). Preach the word; be ready in season and out of season; reprove, rebuke, exhort, with great patience and instruction (2 Tim. 4:2–3).

The elders' shared leadership is especially modeled through team preaching. This benefits the congregation in many ways. They hear the truth of Scripture through various personalities, experience sets, and gifts. They see displayed the deference of the men, one to another. They learn to understand and love their shepherd elders. And they are encouraged to apply their own gifts in service.

Consider the chief purposes of preaching—instructing the people in Biblical truth and exhorting them to use their skills to participate in active service. If one or two men preaching are so occupied with this task, so much so that they neglect other personal ministry, and even their own families, they become negative examples to the congregation. Team preaching relieves each elder of

ASPECTS OF ELDER LEADERSHIP

the heavy burden of weekly sermon preparation, allowing him to also effectively lead in one or more ministries.

The subject matter of what is preached should not be at the discretion of the individual preachers. These choices are the oversight responsibility of the council. The elders should coordinate preaching content so that the people are not exposed to random subjects. Through such thoughtful planning, each brother, when it is his turn, builds on the foundation established previously, thereby demonstrating teamwork, enhancing retention of Biblical content, and encouraging its practical, specific application. This consideration does not preclude a particular man from preaching a series when he is the best choice for that responsibility.

The elders' shared leadership is especially modeled through team preaching.

The emerging leadership gifts of men who are not elders (or not-yet elders), will be surfaced as they are given opportunities to develop their preaching and teaching skills. Any talent available should be counted a blessing. The development of its resources will serve the body over time, producing new leaders. Also, the church will be able to provide elders, preachers, teachers, and leadership to other groups and ministries and prepare for supporting church plants.

The eldership that relies on just one man to do all the teaching must count the cost. Many churches pursue obtaining the very best lead preacher because it is thought his preaching ability is essential to the church's prosperity and progress. But encouraging or just tolerating this thinking is a trap. The man who preaches most of the time may seem to be the de facto senior pastor, or, in time, function as if he is. When everything focuses on one man, an unwholesome, even toxic, dependency relationship with the congregation may develop (a personality cult). Since he dominates the upfront contact and influence with the congregation, it is effectively led by one man with a particular viewpoint. The risks are overwhelming. The damage may even lead to the destruction of the church's Biblical, plural elder governance. And when such men leave for other positions, the churches they vacate often suffer loss of membership and direction. Team preaching is much healthier for the flock.

A *Christianity Today* article entitled, "The Hottest Thing at Church Is Not Your Pastor or Worship Leader," reported that in a 2013 survey by the Gallop Organization, they "found that people in the pews care far more about what's being preached than who's preaching it."[59] The healthy church will be known for the quality of its teaching, its evangelism and discipleship, its ministries to all ages, and its vibrant body life. Its reputation should never be based on the prominence of its one preacher.

The eldership that relies on just one man to do all the teaching must count the cost.

Not all elders need to be (or are) gifted in preaching to large meetings. Some elders may be more effective in a seminar format, an inductive Bible study approach, or in the mentoring of individuals. The most effective discipling and mentoring occurs in smaller groups where interactive give-and-take can occur, and mutual accountability maintained. There is no shortage of the needs and opportunities for such leadership.

The effectiveness of the teacher's work should be judged by the results in the lives of those in his care. Truth be told, retention of Biblical knowledge and applications to life circumstances by those who participate in a small group, inductive Bible study are much greater than for those who sit to hear a sermon. There is no accountability in large group meetings and little retention of content. Just ask one of those who attended for the details of what they learned *and applied* from the sermon of two weeks ago.

Our Valuable Assets

No Biblical or logical reason defends limiting an elder's term of service. Years of front-line experience and demonstrated godly character are the church's invaluable assets. Wise leadership is precious, a treasure not to be squandered or denigrated. We do not set term limits for preachers or commissioned missionaries. Why would we set them for elders?

Understandably, the issue of a man's declining availability for a variety of reasons is to be considered. Compelling and competing time commitments, as well as health and family constraints, often weigh in at some point. The need to keep up with the details of the church's current issues and to attend multiple meetings may not be the best use of the seasoned elder's leadership skills.

Any weakening of the role of elder is avoided when a practical way is found to distinguish between those currently serving on the council and those who served in the past. Many churches have found it appropriate to use the respectful designation *elder emeritus* to refer to that man who has resigned from the council because he is no longer able by virtue of age, health, or unavoidable commitments, to fully fulfill his elder obligations.

The healthy church will be known for the quality of its teaching, its evangelism and discipleship, its ministries to all ages, and its vibrant body life.

Using the term *emeritus* is not the creation of a new office because *emeritus* refers to a person no longer holding a particular position. Such elders no longer have governing responsibility or authority, and are freed from attending numerous meetings so they may make better use of their gifts. If the circumstances preventing such a man from serving on the council change, he may be restored to that responsibility. Also, the concept of elder should not be diluted by using the term elder emeritus as an honorary title for any man who was not previously active in oversight.

Valuable wisdom and discernment are inherent in those who have experienced the church's past history. They have served during its advances and reversals. The neglect of their counsel on contemporary issues is a foolhardy omission. It can even be intentional and is often made by younger, eager elders. Good judgement and common sense call us to depend on the wise elder emeritus for his perspective and advice. He is God's provision for His people. Such godly servants continue to strengthen us, giving us vision and courage.

The fact that these servants continue to shepherd members, as they should, does not change the fact that shepherding alone does not make one an elder. All elders must be shepherds, but not all shepherds are elders. In a healthy body, many people will be involved in shepherding and serving, including the women who are biblically excluded from eldership.

Since elders are appointed by their peer elders, the elder council should periodically confirm and affirm the continuing qualification of their fellows. The full measure of their godly character, as well as their ability to fully participate in council duties and ministry leadership, should be reviewed. The council should establish a procedure whereby each man can assess his situation and assure his colleagues of his willingness and ability to function as a fully active elder. Often, a man's temporary circumstances warrant a short, well-defined furlough.

Good judgement and common sense call on us to depend on the wise elder emeritus for his perspective and advice.

Even as they actively serve on the governing council, elders are responsible for seeing that they are replicated. Their development of young men as leaders and potential elders involves personal mentoring. Joshua's achievements for the Lord were wiped out when his faithful elders died out before he and they had sufficiently mentored and discipled the next generation of elders. The results were terrible for God's people.

> The people served the LORD all the days of Joshua, and all the days of the elders. . . . And there arose another generation after them who did not know the LORD, nor yet the work that He had done for Israel. Then the sons of Israel did evil in the sight of the LORD (Judges 2:7, 10–11).

Again, the training program by Alex Strauch and this author, *The Mentor's Guide to Biblical Eldership,* provides a resource for mentoring potential elders. There the essential Biblical material is studied, and the resources needed for mentoring and evaluating the men aspiring to eldership are provided. Exposure to the actual service and decision-making of the council is key.

The Eldership Community

In *Embracing Shared Leadership*, Joseph Hellerman points out:

> The Bible does not identify a Christian's devotional life as the primary indication of [his] love for God. Nor do personal morality or financial generosity make the cut. Instead, Scripture turns repeatedly to the quality of our relationships—particularly with our fellow Christians—as the foremost evidence of genuine love for God. Jesus put it like this: "'By this all people will know that you are My disciples, if you have love for one another'" (John 13:35).[60]

Elders need to be intentional about building their relationships as brothers. Their fellowship and understanding of each other will fuel their ability to lead the flock. Besides, if they do not demonstrate community among themselves, how can they lead God's people closer to Him? Hellerman again: "Community is the very heart of the Christian faith. And community in our churches must begin at the top."[61]

To model this verity elders would be wise to meet regularly for just fellowship and prayer. At such times the focus should be on their personal lives, the needs of their families, their workplace experiences, and the like. Prayer about congregational matters should be reserved for the elder council's regular meetings. Dealing with essential issues, policy matters, and planning will distract the elders from forming a family of leaders who truly know and love each other, who have formed close relationships. If the elders intend to work together as a team and achieve consensus decisions, they must invest the energy and time in recognizing and respecting each other's viewpoints, backgrounds, and current life concerns, responsibilities, and burdens. Mutual appreciation and comradery can only be achieved in gatherings for fellowship and prayer.

The building of consensus in the council depends on this degree of community among the elders. In their best-selling book, *Getting to Yes*, Roger Fisher and William Ury of the Harvard Negotiation Project point out that the key to obtaining an agreement is consideration of more than a person's stated position. Moving beyond any impasse caused by conflicting and hardened opinions and demands requires discerning the reasoning driving such interests and points of view.[62]

For the eldership council to reach consensus, it is critical that the first effort is placed on mastering our fellow elders' guiding principles and their previous defining experiences. Discernment comes from asking good questions, careful listening, recognition of differing backgrounds, and appreciation of gifts other than one's own—and dedicated effort and time. No man will be persuaded unless he is first understood.

> Speaking the truth *in love*, we are to grow up in all aspects unto Him who is the head, even Christ, from whom the whole body, being fitted and held together by what every joint supplies, according to the proper working of each individual part, causes the growth of the body for the building up of itself *in love* (Eph. 4:15–16, italics added).

Community starts and ends with love.

Conclusion: The Challenge

We must restore the leadership of the church's ministries to home-grown volunteers, including "tent-making" elders. Then we will have once again aligned the structure of the church to the Apostles' intent. The professionalization of church leadership is increasingly destructive and prevents congregational involvement in the exercise of their God-given gifts for ministry. Instead, we should promote our faithful men in their voluntarily service as shepherd leaders. This will inspire and encourage the believers to contribute their personal service and so grow the Church.

We are dealing with a tremendous need to penetrate and leaven today's secular culture. The current trend in the United States is frightening. In January 2018 Barna Research reported:

> It may come as no surprise that the influence of Christianity in the United states is waning. Rates of church attendance, religious affiliation, belief in God, prayer and Bible-reading have been dropping for decades. Americans' beliefs are becoming more post-Christian and, concurrently, religious identity is changing.[63]

We have the choice of being participants in this trend, or we can rise to the leadership challenge. In obedience to the Great Commission, we must mobilize our church members to be out in the world with the

CONCLUSION

light of the gospel. If our fellowships perform like private clubs, we will have failed.

Although our Sunday worship services are important for our spiritual nurture and health, they alone will not equip us to "make disciples of all nations," starting in our own communities. To respond to this summons, we should be employing many varieties of ministry, both in the church and beyond. They must be led by God's servant volunteers, including those that the Holy Spirit is urging to take the helm and govern us as true elders.

The necessary steps for growing these leaders are clear:

- Establish that the Biblical church is a volunteer organization, not a professional, staff-run institution.
- Facilitate and function through volunteer ministry leadership.
- Minimize staff.
- Start developing leaders by encouraging youth to involve themselves in ministry.
- Identify leadership that is being prepared and blessed by the Holy Spirit.
- Provide appropriate training for those potential elders who are exercising ministry leadership.
- Appoint those revealed as Christ's under-shepherds, the leaders responsible to Him, as elders (Heb. 13:17).

SCRIPTURE INDEX

SCRIPTURE INDEX

GENERAL INDEX

GENERAL INDEX

GENERAL INDEX

GENERAL INDEX

About the Author

Richard Swartley obtained his MDiv. from Fuller Theological Seminary in 1959. He is the coauthor with Alexander Strauch of *The Mentor's Guide to Biblical Eldership,* and author of *Eldership in Action: Through Biblical Governance of the Church.* He is coauthor with his wife Anne of *Marriage Preparation: How to Give Couples the Right Start.*

Swartley has over thirty-four years of experience in church leadership as a self-supported elder. His secular fields were satellite communications equipment, and satellite systems engineering. Prior to early retirement in 1994, he managed a sixty-five person satellite communications equipment engineering group, and later on worked as a senior systems engineer for national intelligence systems.

Concurrently, Richard Swartley served as one of the founding elders of what has now become a large, evangelical, non-denominational church in the Northeast. Over the course of his ministry there, he served many years as elder. He continues to serve the Lord as a volunteer, both in the church and without.

Swartley is presently International Coordinator of the translations of the works by Alexander Strauch, published in English in the United States by Lewis and Roth Publishers, a non-profit.

END NOTES

[1] *Christianity That Counts: Being a Christian in a Non-Christian World* (Grand Rapids: Baker Books, 1995), 72–84.

[2] *https://edstetzer.com/2018/06/revitalizing-church-through-an-outward-focus* (accessed 6.1.18).

[3] *https://www.barna.com/research/half-churchgoers-not-heard-great-commission*; updated 3.27.18 (accessed 6.25.18).

[4] 3d ed. (Littleton, CO: Lewis and Roth, 1995).

[5] (Grand Rapids: Kregel, 2013).

[6] (Grand Rapids: Kregel, 2007).

[7] (Dubuque, IA: Emmaus College Press, 2005).

[8] "Just Call Me Curt," *http://exploringthe faith.com/2011/01/14/just-call-me-curt* (accessed 7.28.14).

[9] "Who Should Run the Church? A Case for the Plurality of Elders," *https://bible.org/article/who-should-run-church-case-plurality-elders*; updated 5.24.04 (accessed 8.4.15).

[10] (4.27.00), *http://desiringgod.org/articles/rethinking-the-governance-structure-at-bethlehem-baptist-church*; updated 4.24.00 (accessed 8.4.15).

[11] Biblical Eldership Resources, *http://biblicaleldership.com* (accessed 7.7.18).

[12] Barna Research, "Profile of Protestant Pastors," in Anticipation of Pastor Appreciation Month, *The Barna Update* (9.25.01), 2: *http://www.barna.org/barna-update/article/5-barna-update/59* (accessed 12.29.10).

[13] Trans. Geoffrey W. Bromiley (Grand Rapids: Eerdmans, 1985), 938–39.

[14] E. H. Broadbent, *The Early Church* (London: Pickering and Inglis, 1931).

[15] *https://joshibbardblog.wordpress.com/2016/04/21/calvins-four-church-offices-deacons/#_ftn1* (accessed 6/1/18).

[16] *https://bible.org/article/who-should-run-church-case-plurality-elders*; updated 5.25.04 (accessed 7.7.18).

[17] Poimēn is translated here in Ephesians 4:11correctly in the *English Standard Bible, Youngs Literal Translation,* the *Wycliffe New Testament* and the *English Standard Version* (2016).

[18] *Biblical Eldership,* 303.

END NOTES

[19] Gene A. Getz, *Elders and Leaders: God's Plan for Leading the Church* (Chicago: Moody, 2003), ch. 26; John F. McArthur, *Answering the Key Questions About Elders* (Panorama City, CA: Word of Grace Communications, 2003), ch. 9; (Constitution, Capitol Hill Baptist Church):

> The senior pastor [Mark Dever] shall be an elder. He shall perform the duties of an elder . . . , and shall be recognized by the church as particularly gifted and called to the full-time ministry of preaching and teaching. His call shall not be subject to the triennial reaffirmation or to the term limitation set out in Article 5, Section 2, for elders.

[20] *Questions and Answers by John MacArthur,* 2003 Shepherds' Conference, Grace Community Church, Sun Valley, CA; updated 3.7.03 (accessed 7.7.18).

[21] John MacArthur (Nashville: Nelson Reference & Electronic, 2005), 229.

[22] John Carver and Miriam Mayhew Carver, *Basic Principles of Policy Governance* (San Francisco: Jossey-Bass, 1996).

[23] *http://www.willowcreek .org/governance* (accessed 7.3.18):

> Willow Creek's Elders provide spiritual oversight, direction, and leadership for the overall church, entrusting the implementation of that direction to ministry leaders and staff, under the leadership of the lead pastor.

[24] (IVP Connect; Adapted edition, 1994).

[25] *https://www.nytimes.com/2018/08/08/us/willow-creek-church-resignations-bill-hybels.html* (accessed 8.8.18).

[26] *https://www.christianitytoday.com/2018/august/willow-creek-bill-hybels-heather-larson-elders-resign-inves.html* (accessed 8.8.18).

[27] *The Habits of Highly Effective Churches* (Ventura, CA: Regal, 1999), 37.

[28] *The Compelling Community* (Wheaton: Crossway, 2015), 134, 136.

[29] *Managing People Is Like Herding Cats* (Provo, UT: Executive Excellence Publications, 1999), 163.

[30] *https://www.9marks.org/article/pastors-and-theologians-forum-selecting-elders* (accessed 6.1.18).

[31] *Managing People,* 163.

[32] In 1990, G.E. recognized this accomplishment with the distinction of Division Engineer of the Year.

[33] (San Francisco: Josey-Bass ,1995), 53.

[34] (Colorado Springs: Lewis and Roth, 1996).

[35] (Colorado Springs: Lewis and Roth, 1996).

END NOTES

[36] Stetzer, *https://edstetzer.com* (accessed 6.1.18).

[37] *https://www.nbcnews.com/news/us-news/boy-scouts-america-have-pedophile-epidemic-are-hiding-hundreds-its-n1039661; https://www.denverpost.com/2019/08/04/boy-scout-abuse-colorado-lawsuit; https://scoutmastercg.com/bsa-ends-the-ban-on-gay-leaders/* (accessed 8.11.19).

[38] Christian Camp and Conference Association, *info.ccca.org.*

[39] *https://www.thegospelcoalition.org/article/9-ways-to-raise-up-leaders-in-your-church* (accessed 6.1.18).

[40] *The First Epistle of Clement to the Corinthians,* 44.3 *Early Christian Writings: The Apostolic Fathers*, tr. Maxwell Staniforth (New York: Dorset Press, 1986), 46.

[41] Swartley, *Eldership in Action*, 50–53; revised.

[42] Larry Osborne, *The Unity Factor: Developing a Healthy Church Leadership Team* (Vista, CA: Owl's Nest, 1989), 42–45.

[43] *The Power of Team Leadership* (Colorado Springs: WaterBrook, 2001), 26.

[44] Alexander Strauch, *Paul's Vision for the Deacons: Assisting the Elders with the Care of God's Church* (Colorado Springs: Lewis and Roth, 2017).

[45] *The Power of Team Leadership*, 24.

[46] *How to Make Meetings Work* (New York: Jove, 1982), 183–85.

[47] Blenko, Mankins, and Rogers, *Decide and Deliver: Five Steps to Breakthrough Performance in Your Organization* (Boston: Harvard Business Review Press, 2010), 88.

[48] *Organizational Behavior*, 8th ed. (Upper Saddle River, NJ: Prentice Hall, 1997), 260.

[49] *Biblical Eldership*, 47.

[50] *Collected Writings of John Murray: Lectures in Systematic Theology* (Carlisle, PA: Banner of Truth, reprint 1991), 346.

[51] *https://en.wikipedia.org/wiki/Groupthink*; updated 6.8.18 (accessed 7.7.18).

[52] Carver and Carver, *Basic Principles.*

[53] Swartley, *Eldership in Action,* 78.

[54] *Leading from the Sandbox* (Colorado Springs: NavPress, 2010), 40.

[55] *Brothers, We Are Not Professionals: A Plea to Pastors for Radical Ministry* (Nashville: B&H Publishers Group), 1.

[56] *http://mikeslaughter.com/blog/paid-staff-versus-unpaid-servants*; updated 2.21.16 (accessed 7.9.18).

END NOTES

[57] Dever and Dunlop, *The Compelling Community*, 137.

[58] *The Habits of Highly Effective Churches*, 36.

[59] *www.christianitytoday.com/news/2017/april/gallup-hottest-thing-at-church-not-pastor-worship.html* (accessed 7.10.18).

[60] (Grand Rapids: Kregel Press, 2013), 282.

[61] Ibid, 284.

[62] (New York: Penguin Books, 1991).

[63] *https://www.barna.com/research/atheism-doubles-among-generation-z* (accessed 12.23.18).

www.ingramcontent.com/pod-product-compliance
Lightning Source LLC
Chambersburg PA
CBHW071020040426
42443CB00007B/863